101 THINGS TO DO AT UNIVERSITY

Crombie Jardine Publishing Limited
Office 2, 3 Edgar Buildings
George Street
Bath BA1 2FJ
www.crombiejardine.com

First published by Crombie Jardine
Publishing Limited, 2008
Copyright © Crombie Jardine
Publishing Limited, 2008
ISBN: 978-1-906051-27-3

Design and typesetting by Mathew Lyons
Printed in the UK by CPI William Clowes
Beccles NR34 7TL

The Author

After surviving numerous 'dirty pints'[1] and 'all-nighters', Lel Moss graduated from Loughborough University with a BA and MA before beginning her PhD, which she hopes to finish some day. She has also worked as a lecturer at several universities and is currently deciding which degree to do next.

---

1. See no. 65, page 88

Acknowledgements

Lel Moss would like to thank Dr Jonathan Taylor without whom she would not have achieved her first degree; her family Geoff, Jenny and Vicky and friends Tim and Sarah for their continual support; and her fellow students from Loughborough University for their influence and inspiration.

*The university brings out all abilities
including incapability.*
Anton Chekhov

Disclaimer:
*This is a light-hearted guide
offering both sound and irresponsible
'advice' and the publishers accept
no responsibility whatsoever for anyone
without a sense of humour following
this advice to the letter.*

Contents

Introduction

101 Things to Do at University aims to provide you with an unpretentious, witty and mischievous guide whether you are soon to be starting or soon to be finishing university.

There are numerous guides available for first-time students which focus on entry scores, league tables and staff/student ratios. Although invaluable when choosing your university, these handbooks often omit the humorous and unmentionable events of the average student experience. *101 Things to Do at University* aims to bridge this gap by offering a facetious look at student life, making reference to the many unspoken ceremonies, rituals and initiations which you will undertake during your time as a student.

The guide is based on thorough research and has been compiled from authentic experiences from students, young and old. The book covers most aspects of student life and is organised into eight sections: Finance, Academia, Health and Hygiene, Accommodation,

Relationships, Drinking, The Student Union, and Graduation.

Graduates will recognise many of these offerings whilst those who are about to begin their university experience will have their appetites whetted and their fear levels raised…

Finance

1. Apply for a student loan

Even if your parents pay for your fees, accommodation and living costs, it is imperative that you apply for a student loan. Student loans should not be thought of in the same way as bank loans. Firstly, you will not start repaying these until you have reached a certain salary threshold, which you should not anticipate to do for several years. Secondly, when you finally begin repayments they will be so small that you will scarcely notice them. Please note that your student loan will never be in your bank account on the prearranged date and you will most likely spend around £30 on phone costs calling the SLC (Student Loan Company) chasing up your loan. On the arrival of your loan it is customary that you spend it wholly within two weeks of receipt.[1]

---

1. Editor's Note: Don't do it.

2. Befriend your student bank advisor

The student bank advisor is an important person to befriend. It can sometimes be advantageous if they are of the opposite sex. If not, you should embark on some minor stalking to learn their hobbies and preferred drinking establishments in order to generate meeting opportunities. A good rapport with your student bank advisor is essential when requesting an increase on your overdraft when you have spent your student loan and when you want to go on holiday to Amsterdam. If your new friend refuses to increase your overdraft you are permitted to sob, shriek and collapse in the bank and if this fails you should apply for a student credit card.

3. Ask for student discount

You will hastily discover that the 10% student discount is arguably one of the leading perks of being a student and it is therefore crucial that you request a discount in every business you visit. Whilst many high street shops do offer this bonus as standard, it is essential that you ask for a discount even when you are aware that the response will be an uncompromising 'no'. Try requesting a discount in the following places:

- ✔ betting shops
- ✔ post offices
- ✔ banks
- ✔ charity shops
- ✔ libraries

4. Avoid fruit machines

Fruit machines are ingeniously but cruelly located near the cash machine in most Student Unions.

Your initial encounter with one may merely be to occupy a pint whilst waiting for a friend. Nevertheless, be prepared for an addiction to commence and for a considerable percentage of your student loan to be wasted. You should aim to avoid fruit machines at all costs. If you are partial to gambling and are in need of some swift money you should seek something with considerably better odds such as the local bingo.

5. Buy a big toy

With your student loan recently in your bank account and your new student credit card in your pocket it is probable that you will experience the urge to overindulge on one big purchase. This purchase is commonly something you have wanted since a child and as a result is typically a big toy. Moreover, in a traditional childlike manner you will play with your new toy non-stop for the first week and be disinterested in it by the second. Some common examples of big toy purchases include:

- ✔ a professional size snooker table
- ✔ a karaoke machine
- ✔ a giant indoor paddling pool
- ✔ an oversized 'Scalextric'
- ✔ a remote control plane
- ✔ professional walkie talkies

6. Lose your accommodation deposit

Whether you are in halls of residence or in a rented house you will have to pay a deposit. It is imperative that you do not consider this money as a deposit as you will more than likely never see this money again. Proceedings such as house parties and particulars such as giant indoor paddling pools will almost certainly destroy your walls and carpets and as a result few landlords anticipate returning accommodation deposits to students.

7. Shop in a charity shop

Throughout your time at university you will come to appreciate how valuable charity shops are to the student experience. Charity shops should be your only stop when you require fancy dress clothing, second-hand text books, stationery and inexpensive birthday presents for your friends. Don't forget to ask for a student discount.

8. Apply to the hardship fund

Following your big toy purchases and despite shopping in a charity shop it is probable that you will find it necessary to apply to the university hardship fund. Hardship fund grants are for students who experience unanticipated financial difficulties and to obtain one such grant, applicants must demonstrate how and why this has occurred. To do this, the university will require copies of your bank statements for the previous six months which is where the problems arise for the average student. Your chances of success are significantly improved if your statements do not contain payments to any of the following places:

✗ online gambling websites
✗ off-licences
✗ nightclub bars
✗ lavish holiday websites
✗ sex-chat phone lines

9. Seek part-time employment

Seeking part-time employment will not be your foremost priority when reaching university but there are in fact numerous benefits in obtaining work. Firstly, jobs are easy to attain as students are inexpensive and are willing work for the minimum wage. Secondly, your parents may be pleasantly surprised with the exertion you are making and may therefore be more likely to offer you money. Finally, if you gain employment in a bar, sweetshop, or off-licence you will normally receive a staff discount which you can then offer to your friends. It is imperative that you attempt as many diverse jobs as possible during your time at university. Aim for at least two a year to avoid the ensuing boredom and to avoid being detected for the complimentary drinks and sweets you frequently provide your friends with.

10. Volunteer for social science experiments

The majority of universities with a department of social sciences will advertise for students to volunteer for research experiments. Tests can range from eating chocolate until you feel unwell to running on a tread mill until you pass out. Tests can be tedious, emotional and occasionally cruel but you will generally be compensated for your attendance. Some departments offer money which is often equal to the minimum wage. Some tests require you to eat which in turn means a complimentary lunch, whilst some departments offer free tickets to events at the Student Union. A regular volunteer can make a good income from such experiments and you should endeavour to do these twice a month.

11. Make a begging call to your parents

With your student loan, overdraft and credit card all in the red and your food cupboard bare you will be required to phone your parents to request some money. This is commonly referred to among students as the 'begging call' and undoubtedly it will not be the last one that you will make whilst at university. It is crucial that you practise your speech before calling home. For some, the following phrases have proven successful:

I didn't realise the books would be so expensive.
I've only eaten two slices of bread in the last week.
My shoes have got holes in them.
I need new glasses.

Academia

12. Befriend your lecturers

Lecturers on first appearance appear old, unexciting and generally in need of a dirty pint but on the inside the majority of lecturers are like you. In all probability they spent their student days undertaking pub golf challenges, skinny dipping in fountains and stealing road signs and as a result they are often uncomplicated to befriend. It is constructive to befriend your lecturer as you never know when you may need an extension on your assignment or extra assistance with your dissertation.

13. Befriend the department secretary

A department secretary is surprisingly one of the most authoritative people in the whole university. Department secretaries have the power to lose your medical notes when you need an extension, reject your assignment when it is submitted one minute late and miscalculate your exam grades. It is therefore beneficial to befriend this person. A box of chocolates or a bottle of wine at the end of your first year should be enough to ensure that they are pleasant to you for the remainder of your degree.

14. Buy a considerable amount of books

It is an undisclosed fact that you will never read many of the books that are on your reading list. You will spend approximately £300 a year purchasing these books and some will remain, throughout your entire degree, on your shelf in the shrink-wrap you bought them in. This occurs for a number of reasons. Firstly, lecturers list their own books as essential purchases on their reading lists. They do this to make money and their books are often irrelevant to your degree. Secondly, you will be able to gain a lot of information regarding your course in an abbreviated format on the internet. Moreover, you will be able to get an old edition of your book from the library in which a kindly fellow student has previously highlighted the key parts.

15. Visit the university bookshop

You must ensure that you visit the university bookshop in freshers' week when staff are at their busiest and are most stressed. It is imperative that you do not buy any books from there, but that you waste their time enquiring about a book on some taboo topic such as bestiality. If they can oblige with your book request, it is essential that you do not buy the book and before you depart you must inform staff that books are cheaper to buy on the internet.

16. Visit the library

Outside of the Student Union, the university library is widely considered as the social hub of the university. This occurs for several reasons. Firstly, the library is always warm which is favourable when you have not paid your gas or electricity bill. Secondly, the library is an excellent location to flirt with members of the opposite sex. Finally, the library often stocks DVDs and CDs for media and music courses. These items should be borrowed (for free) and then illegally copied.

17. Attend guest lectures

Whilst you are walking around university you should constantly be aware of posters advertising guest lectures. Guest lectures, as expected, are habitually monotonous and extremely long. However, there are generally hidden incentives to attract students to such events. Firstly, they offer the ideal opportunity to befriend your lecturers. To your lecturer you will appear engrossed in your subject and as a result they will think well of you.

Secondly, and most significantly, guest lectures are often followed by free food and wine and as these lectures generally take place on campus they are the ideal warm-up to a night at the Student Union.

18. Experience an all-nighter

An 'all-nighter' is the technical term for staying up all night to complete an assignment. Typically, the assignment will need to be submitted by 9am and on average you will have had at least five weeks to write it. An all-nighter is a gruelling activity but you should aim to experience it before each assessment deadline. Necessary equipment for an all-nighter includes:

- ✔ caffeine drinks
- ✔ caffeine drugs
- ✔ snacks
- ✔ DVDs
- ✔ social networking websites

19. Revise

The experience of revising at university can be compared to that of an all-nighter. However, preparation for such an event generally begins in advance. It is crucial that all female students draw colourful revision timetables which take at least two days to construct. Such timetables will never be kept to. In contrast, male students should think of revision preparation as a group activity because you will usually want to meet up in the Student Union to discuss revision techniques and exam tactics. Both of these preparation methods will prove fruitless and on average revision usually occurs on the morning before the exam.

20. Lose your work on your computer

Whether you are writing an extensive begging letter to your parents or an assignment which is due in the following day, you should on at least one occasion lose your work on your computer. If this type of loss frequently occurs you will believe that you have a strong argument to request a new computer from your parents.

21. Misunderstand postgraduates

As an undergraduate student you may on occasion meet a postgraduate. Postgraduate students are usually doing a Masters or a PhD degree and you will presume, quite rightly, that they must be boring, friendless and highly intelligent. However, you will come to realise that postgraduates are students who simply do not want to get a job and want to exist as a student for the foreseeable future. As you prepare to leave university you may even envy such students and consider a postgraduate degree for yourself.

Health and Hygiene

22. Catch freshers' flu

Catching freshers' flu in approximately the second or third week of your first year is a rite of passage for every student. Freshers' flu can be defined as a condition in which a student fears they have contracted a life threatening virus, when in reality they are merely suffering the effects of two weeks of excessive drinking, eating and a lack of sleep. Freshers' flu can be identified by the following symptoms:

- ✔ a sore throat (which has nothing to do with the continual shouting and singing you have undertaken)
- ✔ vomiting (which has nothing to do with the eleven pints you have consumed)
- ✔ earache (which has nothing to do with standing beside a speaker in the Union for three hours)

Please note that although this condition is called freshers' flu, all students must attempt to contract this virus every year to reconfirm their student status.

23. Visit accident and emergency

Throughout your time at university it is probable that you or/and your friends will visit your local accident and emergency for any number of drink related injuries. You should endeavour to visit at least twice a year, either for yourself or your friends. The most common complaints will be:

✔ alcohol poisoning
✔ broken noses
✔ broken legs
✔ pregnancy test
✔ oven burns

24. Catch a sexually transmitted disease[1]

If you are fortunate enough to have sex at university, you must try and catch a sexually transmitted disease. By doing this you will not only prove to those around you that you

---

1. Editor's Note: Don't do it.

had sex but also that you did it for long enough to catch something. If you are struggling to attract the opposite sex, you could try and contract herpes or scabies from towels at the laundrette or gym.

25. Experience severe sunburn

As you reach your first spring term at university you will observe that students do not wear sunscreen. Firstly, this is because sunscreen costs money and secondly because sunscreen gets in the way of achieving a tan. On the rare occasion when there is sun on campus you must without delay wear the minimum of clothing and sunbathe. You should aim to have severe sunburn and mild sunstroke by the end of the afternoon[1] so that when you are in the Student Union you will not need many drinks before you feel drunk. Sunscreen should only be worn if an attractive member of the opposite sex is offering to apply it.

---

1. Editor's Note: Use sunscreen!

26. Collect medical notes

If you are unwell with a broken
nose, freshers' flu or a simple oven
burn it is imperative that you visit
the university doctor and request a
medical note. Medical notes can
cost money but at university surger-
ies they are often free. Medical
notes are a priceless commodity to
possess as a student and you should
aim to have a small store of these
for emergencies. You never know
when you may require an extension
on your coursework or when you
may need to claim there were

extenuating circumstances which caused you to fail your exam.

27. Gain weight

Before you arrive at university you must be prepared to gain weight. It is imperative that you gain at least a stone in your first year and that when your clothes become tight you do not buy any new ones. For female students this will generate a condition called the overhang, whilst male students will gradually develop a small pot-belly which is commonly referred to as a studo.

Some widespread causes of an over-hang and a studo are:

✔ alcopops (which surprisingly contain five hundred calories)
✔ chips (which will accompany every meal you consume)
✔ all-nighters (which usually result in all night snacking)

28. Join the university gym

The university gym should not be used for undertaking exercise, but it is vital that you join every year. Your gym membership should only be used for access to the jacuzzi, steam room, sauna, sun bed and in general for looking at members of the opposite sex. The gym is also a fine place to take a hot shower when your housemates have used all of the hot water.

29. Walk

Before your arrival at university you should prepare your body for the colossal amount of walking which you will undertake. As a student, taxis are only to be used for special occasions or in emergencies such as rain, broken legs and making last orders at the pub. For the majority of students walking will be the only form of exercise and as studies show that walking can reduce body fat and enhance your mental well-being, you should think of it as a positive activity.

30. Wash your clothes

It is probable that your arrival at university will be your first time away from home and as a result it is likely that you will have never washed your own clothes. Washing clothes at university is not straight-forward and there are numerous challenges set before the common student. Firstly, university laundrettes are absurdly overpriced. Secondly, you will require washing powder which in addition costs money. Finally, it is probable that you will shrink your much-loved jeans or dye your treasured shirt. Ensure that you make washing a once a term event and if you urgently require something clean it may be simpler to buy more clothes.

31. Wash your bed linen

In a similar way to the washing of clothes, bed linen should also be washed very rarely. Certain situations such as vomiting may result in the need for more regular washing. However, unlike clothing, duvet and pillow covers can be turned inside out to attain another month of usage. As before, if washing your bed linen creates an aggravation, merely buy more bed linen as required.

32. Dress like a student

For the majority of your time at university you will be cold. This is not merely due to your unpaid gas and electricity bills but because the most common student clothing consists of shorts and flip-flops. These items are usually coupled with some university stash and must be worn all through the year even when it snows.

33. Experiment with your hair

With their newly acquired student status, a large majority of students will adopt a new hairstyle. University is the ideal time to experiment with your hair as there are numerous student discounts available in local hairdressers. For male students your new style will usually involve bleaching or shaving, whilst female students should prepare to go to the opposite spectrum of their natural hair colour. Blondes will become brunettes and vice versa.

Accommodation

34. Experience hall rivalry

Within most universities you will commonly find passionate rivalry between different halls of residence. As a result, you must ensure that you are excessively patriotic about your hall and raucously offensive about others. There are traditionally songs which will be sung when experiencing hall rivalry and it is your duty to learn these.

35. Host a house party

You must only host a house party if you possess the full knowledge of what to expect. You must anticipate that your house will look like a bomb site and that your accommodation deposit will be lost within an hour of the party starting. You must also warn your neighbours about your party and offering a bottle of wine as a sweetener is highly recommended. House parties most commonly have a theme such as a beach party which involves bikinis, shorts and sangria. Another popular theme is a letter party where students dress in a costume beginning with a certain letter. For example, for a 'T' party, guests could dress as tennis players, top gun pilots and testicles.

36. Cook an end of term feast

Before you return home for the summer, your landlord will hand you a full list of instructions before leaving the property. One of these instructions will most likely read: 'All fridges and freezers must be emptied.' As you are a student and now live by the rule that in no circumstances should food be thrown away, you and your fellow housemates are expected to cook an end of term feast. The feast involves the consumption of the entire contents of the fridge (generally ignoring best-by dates) and cooking the entire contents of the freezer. The most common feasts feature:

- ✔ coleslaw
- ✔ frozen vegetables
- ✔ frozen sausage rolls
- ✔ cauliflower cheese
- ✔ mayonnaise

37. Watch daytime television

With the average student having in the region of twelve hours of lessons a week, and only in fact attending half of these, you should not be surprised to discover that you will in all probability develop an addiction to daytime television. The signs of an addiction are easy to identify. The addict may start lying and making excuses to leave lunch early to avoid missing an episode or they may even, in worse-case scenarios, carry their remote control around with them. The most common causes of a daytime television addiction are:

- ✔ *Neighbours* (because it is a national institution)
- ✔ *Diagnosis Murder* (for the man who was in *Mary Poppins*)
- ✔ *Jeremy Kyle* (to laugh at Chavs)
- ✔ *Bargain Hunt* (for David 'the Duke' Dickinson)

38. Play computer games

For approximately one week each term, the majority of male students will develop a group addiction to a computer game. These are typically football manager games but numerous varieties exist. The infatuation will result in entire weeks when addicts do not leave their rooms except to use the toilet or to collect their takeaways from the door. Addicts generally gather in one room, which will be constantly warm and musty, and where the curtains will be drawn.

39. Buy a pet hamster or goldfish

It is essential that either you or one of your fellow housemates buys a hamster or a goldfish. These are the only two officially recognised pets for students as they do not live too long and they are largely low maintenance. However, you must ensure that you spend a ludicrous sum of money on a space-age cage or a high-tech aquarium for your new companion. When approaching the first university holiday you must rigorously negotiate with your housemates for ownership of the pet, but by the second university holiday you must draw straws to see who gets lumbered with it.

40. Put up traditional student posters

The majority of the walls which you will live within as a student will be white, and with landlords banning most forms of decoration it is likely that you will decorate your walls with posters. However, it is crucial that your chosen posters can be classed as student posters. Some popular student posters include images of:

✔ The Simpsons
✔ mountains

✔ surfers
✔ porn stars
✔ road signs

41. Make a photo-wall

It is to be expected that you will take numerous photographs with your newly purchased (with overdraft) digital camera. The majority of such photographs will never be printed but those rare and special ones that are should be placed in one big mass on your wall called a photo-wall. You will look at these photos during your degree as you increasingly gain weight, shave and/or dye your hair and progressively look unwell. You will also look at these as a finalist and think how young you looked.

42. Use the internet

Increasingly, the majority of halls of residence come with free internet access and for your entire time in halls full advantage of this should be taken. For male students this will regularly involve downloading porn and illegal movies and music. For female students this will commonly involve ordering clothes, perfume and cosmetics from various discount websites twenty-four hours a day.

43. Befriend your cleaners

When you are in halls of residence it is probable that you will have a cleaner who visits your room daily to empty your bin and weekly to clean it. Cleaners are often female and mature and for understandable reasons they dislike students. However, no matter how discourteous or noisy your cleaner is, you should attempt to befriend her. Buy her a box a chocolates at Christmas or some flowers as a thank you in the spring. It should be acknowledged that befriended cleaners have in the past cooked for and cleaned the clothes and bed linen of their preferred students.

44. Make a house cleaning rota

Whether you are a female or you live with females it is highly likely that you will come across a legendary house cleaning rota. House cleaning rotas are typically constructed in the first week of the year and are always ignored by the end of the second.

45. Wash up

The washing of plates and cutlery should be thought of in the same way as the washing of clothes and bed linen. Washing up should only be done when it is absolutely essential. Even then, you should only wash an item when it is needed. Please note that you will always need to buy new cutlery each year as it is habitually prone to theft.

46. Block a toilet

Blocked toilets are usually the result of too much human waste, toilet tissue, various different cosmetic and feminine items. Toilets can also be blocked by flushing down the remains of an end of term feast. As plumbers routinely charge in the region of £100 to look at a toilet, students should buy a plunger and draw straws. If a plunger does not work it is recommended that you use a coat hanger, hockey stick or somebody else's cutlery to dislodge the blockage. In no circumstances should a plumber be called.

47. Experience the fire alarm

You should prepare yourself to hear the fire alarm at least once a week in your first year at university. This is largely because students set off alarms for fun when they are drunk or students forget they have started cooking something (usually when drunk). Female students will repeatedly take pleasure in the chance to flirt with a fireman whilst male students will aim to time fire alarms at night to see female students in their nightdresses and to observe who comes out of whose room.

48. Go food shopping

Visiting a large supermarket is a hazardous affair as a student. On the surface you are going with the intention of buying food which is an essential part of life. Nevertheless, when you arrive you will be compelled to buy DVDs, CDs and even TVs. Please note that the only food you will purchase will be a big bag of pasta, some crisps and numerous bottles of low-cost cider.

49. Eat pasta

Whether you take pleasure in eating it or not, pasta will become a staple part of your diet as a student and you should endeavour to consume it at least four times a week. The popularity of pasta is due to the fact that it is cheap, quick to cook and incredibly versatile. The most common student pasta dishes are:

✔ tuna mayo pasta
✔ cheesy pasta
✔ tomato sauce pasta
✔ pasta, beans and cheese
✔ chilli pasta

50. Steal food

Theft is not acceptable in most walks of life, but as a student you are legally entitled and expected to steal food from your fellow housemates or neighbours. You should challenge yourself to cook a fry-up ensuring that every item has been 'donated' by a different person.

Please note that you are absolutely permitted to be enraged if a fellow student steals food from you.

51. Start a kitchen fire

The kitchen is where the most fires occur in the home and in student accommodation this rule is no exception. However, within student accommodation the majority of fires occur between 11pm and 4am linking these fires almost certainly to alcohol. The most common causes of student fires include:

✘ drying clothes in the microwave
✘ hanging tea towels to dry over
   the cooker
✘ chip pan fryers[1]

Relationships

52. Make friends with everyone

The first week of university is the time to meet people and with newly found confidence you will in all probability make approximately

---

1. Editor's Note: Stay away from the kitchen when you are drunk!

ten new friends a day. It is important to note that a small but elite assortment of these friends will remain your friends for life, whilst you will never speak to the majority again after you've graduated.

53. Be given a nickname

Your new status as a student will habitually come with a new name as most students adopt or are given an absurd nickname in freshers' week. Your new title will remain with you throughout the next three years and will even permeate into the workplace. The majority of university nicknames are inventively created by adding a 'y' to the end of your surname such as 'Mossy', 'Woody' and 'Welshy'. Moreover, some names are merely related to your home town, for example: 'Scouse Dave', 'Brummie Pete' and 'Geordie Rob'.

54. Join social networking websites

During freshers' week you will promptly realise that social networking websites are vital when surviving the average student day. You must ensure that you log in at least once an hour to keep up to date with last night's photographs and tonight's plans. Moreover, you will almost certainly feel exceptionally popular with hundreds of names on your friends lists despite the fact you have only met a handful of them.

55. Go on a student holiday

As you achieve the superior status of a second or third year student it is probable that your friendship group will book a holiday. Such holidays are likely to be in Europe and

Amsterdam is an understandable and popular choice. However, you must ensure that you preserve the traditions of a student holiday by staying in a run-down hostel in the middle of the red light district. It is essential that no one must admit that they would rather book into a pleasant three star hotel even though it is evident that you are all thinking it. It is also vital that one of your friends must get arrested, one must have a lesbian/gay experience and one must have alcohol poisoning for it to be considered an authentic student holiday.

56. Tell gap year stories

As a large percentage of students now embark upon gap year travels before starting university you will as a result accumulate dozens of what you believe to be interesting and witty stories about your time in Thailand, Australia or New Zealand. Upon your arrival at university your head will be filled with such tales and as a result you will almost always bore your new friends to the point when gap year stories are prohibited.

57. Use university lingo

With your new nickname, your new clothing and excessive pride in your university, it is vital that you start to use new words. Most universities have common terms and phrases which you must ensure you learn from finalists and then pass on to freshers before you graduate. Some common examples and their meanings include:

Eat it fresh – Down your drink
Are you on the lash? – Are you going out tonight?

Who is that randomer? – Who is that stranger?
He is a bit Charles – He is stereotypically upper class

58. Insult freshers

Having successfully survived your first year at university it is accepted that you will acquire a certain degree of arrogance. Moreover, as you go into your second year you will develop an uncontrollable urge to insult freshers. You will stare at such students and mutter phrases such as 'I never did that' and 'Who do they think they are?' You will also consider how young they look and you will reflect that you never looked or acted that immaturely.

59. Insult neighbouring universities

Whether you are a student in a big city or a small town it is imperative that you insult neighbouring universities. Friendly sports matches are regularly organised between local universities and such occasions present an ideal opportunity to taunt rival students about how your university is superior in every way.

60. Have a long distance relationship

If you have the pleasure of attending a different university to your boyfriend or girlfriend, it is essential that you swear to your new friends that you are both deeply in love and that you will stay loyal to him or her throughout your years at university. It is likely that they will call for a bet on this declaration and you must oblige. It is also important that you apologise accordingly to your new friends when you cheat on him or her in freshers' week and subsequently call off the relationship. All bets should be paid promptly.

61. Have a student relationship

A student relationship is dissimilar to a regular relationship and for this reason the majority do not survive when you graduate from university. The student relationship can be identified by the following attributes:

✘ not talking to each other unless you are drunk
✘ fighting at around 11pm each night
✘ you do not know anything about each other's family or friends

✘ you don't see each other during
   university holidays
✘ he/she leaves before you wake
   up in the morning

62. Make a hall incest chart

When male and female students
live in confined spaces it is highly
probable that there will be numerous student relationships. As you all
know each other well and you
rarely remain with the same person
for more than two weeks, these
relationships will often be termed
as incest. It is highly recommended

that you create a chart which reflects how students have been related in halls. Different colour lines should be used to denote different levels of intimacy. The incest chart is also a practical tool when tracing the origins of a sexually transmitted disease.

Drinking

63. Buy the cheapest alcohol

To profit from the increase in binge drinking, supermarkets are producing cheaper alcohol. It is your duty as a student to ensure that you seek out the cheapest alcohol obtainable.

64. Open a bottle

It is imperative that during your time as a student you do not open a bottle using a bottle opener. Using a bottle opener is too easy and as a university student with your enhanced intelligence, you and your friends must strive to develop new methods of bottle opening. Some methods to try to include:

✔ with your teeth
✔ against a radiator
✔ with another bottle
✔ with clenched bum cheeks

65. Consume a dirty pint

A dirty pint is a cruel but celebrated fluid at universities. Students should expect to drink a dirty pint on special occasions such as birthdays, initiations and to mark the end of exams. Key ingredients for a dirty pint include:

✔ any spirit
✔ any lager or bitter

✔ anything that curdles such as Irish Cream Liqueur

It is recommended that the dirty pint should be consumed outdoors or next to a toilet as vomiting is customary.

66. Make alcohol jelly

The making of alcohol jelly tends to be a female student activity and these jellies will habitually be found at female house parties. Nevertheless, both male and female students should aim to consume approximately fifty each year to confirm their student status. Alcohol jellies should not be thought of as real alcohol as they are consumed in the form of food. The most popular mixtures include:

✔ vodka with strawberry jelly
✔ absinthe with lime jelly
✔ whisky with cola jelly
✔ white rum with mango jelly
✔ tequila with orange jelly

67. Go on a bar crawl

Upon your arrival at university, you should endeavour to take part in regular bar crawls. There are numerous types of bar crawls which you must attempt as a student and crucially each type has its own theme, customs, rules and costumes. Some key examples to research and try to include:

✔ pub golf
✔ three legged
✔ Monopoly
✔ alphabet
✔ cross dressing

68. Drinking games

Drinking games are a traditional component of the student experience and as a result the majority of universities have their own long-established games. It is important to note that some games will require apparatus such as an empty pint glass, a pack of cards or a penny and it is your responsibility to be prepared for such occasions. Moreover, it is your duty to learn and practise these games regularly to pass them on to freshers when you reach your final year. Some common student drinking games to research and try are:

✔ Thumb master
✔ 5's
✔ Fuzzy duck
✔ 21
✔ Ring of fire

69. Collect shot glasses

With each single shot of alcohol that you consume at university you will feel increasing pride and as a result it is common for students to steal their cherished shot glass from the bar as proof of their accomplishment. Empty shot glasses should then be constructed into a pyramid shape in your window as verification of your student status to any passers-by. Please note that a pyramid can also be created with beer cans, but this does tend to block out daylight.

70. Consume a strawpedo

A strawpedo is effectively a drinking race and it is created by placing a straw in a bottle of alcopop and bending the top over the peak of the bottle to allow air to enter. This action creates a torpedo effect as the drink travels through the straw and into your mouth at a great speed. As a beginner you may find this skill difficult to master but it is important that you aim to improve your speed throughout your time at university. Some respectable times to aim for are:

- ✔ 1st Year – 5.1 seconds
- ✔ 2nd Year – 3.8 seconds
- ✔ 3rd Year – 2.9 seconds

71. Fight with a townie

A townie is the name given to inhabitants of a university town. Townies, as they are collectively named, will generally be annoyed that you live in their town and that you repeatedly cause havoc. As a result you should expect to be in a fight with a townie at least once a year. Please note that it is not uncommon for small riots to occur between university rugby teams and large groups of townies.

72. Lose your mobile phone

With the remainder of your over-draft it is expected that you will buy the latest mobile phone and it is increasingly likely that you will have lost or damaged your new phone within a month. This will almost certainly occur during an evening of strawpedos and dirty pints and as a rule occurs the day after you have cancelled your mobile phone insurance. The most common causes of student mobile phone loss and damage include said item:

✘ being left in a taxi
✘ being dropped down the toilet
✘ being dropped in a pint
✘ being thrown at a wall after a fight with your boyfriend or girlfriend

73. Experience an alcohol vomit

Alcohol vomiting plays a fundamental role in every student experience. It is an unavoidable certainty that it will occur at least once a week and on average you should aim to vomit in at least five of the following places to confirm your student status:

- ✔ your bed
- ✔ somebody else's bed
- ✔ by a fire exit in the Student Union
- ✔ on the Student Union dance floor
- ✔ on the Student Union bar
- ✔ on a fruit machine
- ✔ on the closed lid of a toilet
- ✔ in your pint glass
- ✔ in someone's coat hood
- ✔ against the window of a kebab shop

74. Steal road signs

It is conceivably one of the oldest student clichés but the stealing of road signs, university signs and traffic cones is a major component in your initiation into student status. When drunk and walking home from an evening out, prepare to be suddenly overcome with the urge to acquire a little memento of the night. The majority of universities have cherished signs such as a university welcome sign. These are often complicated to steal as they have been repeatedly nailed down by university security. Nevertheless, you must attempt to steal this prized sign on regular occasions.

75. *Steal a shopping trolley*

In a comparable approach to the stealing of road signs, the stealing of a shopping trolley is a student rite of passage. Supermarkets had tried to overturn this trend by introducing coin deposits and it is therefore crucial that you ensure you have saved some money for your walk home. Unlike road signs, shopping trolleys should only be thought of as a temporary memento of the night. However, they are useful for racing, carrying takeaways and pushing your friends to A&E.

76. Eat a 2am takeaway

The drunken 2am takeaway is not a student-specific trend but it is a must if you intend to develop the required weight gain for your new student status. The most common foods include:

✔ pizza
✔ chips and cheese

✔ kebabs (without salad)
✔ burgers (without salad)
✔ curry

Please note that all items should be accompanied with mayonnaise.

77. Experience a long walk home

It is imperative that when walking home from an evening out you make a journey that should usually take twenty minutes last two hours. This is a condition called the long walk home and it is not known why and how time passes so slowly.

Please note that the long walk home has nothing to do with the queue in the takeaway, various toilet stops and the road sign and shopping trolley stealing you perform en route.

78. Wake up with food on your pillow

Waking up with food on your pillow is a disturbing event but one which every student will experience during their time at university. The experience involves waking up with the remains of your drunken 2am takeaway on your pillow. It is habitually a foul experience and can be extremely messy if you ordered a curry.

The Student Union

79. Compete in the Student Union pub quiz

On Sunday nights the majority of universities run a pub quiz and it is imperative that you attend this weekly. There are usually benefits to entice students. Firstly, the drinks are typically cheap and secondly the prizes are usually monetary. Please note that your chances of winning are greatly increased if one of your friends remains at home with the internet to text you the required answers.

80. Develop a love of cheesy music

When you begin your time at university your MP3 player will reflect your individual musical tastes whether they are blackened death metal or progressive trance. However, within three months your tastes will have changed and you will begin to take pleasure from the universal student genre of cheese. Soon artists such as S Club 7, Chesney Hawkes and Hanson will be regulars on your play list and Bryan Adams' *Summer of '69* will often be on repeat.

81. Celebrate seasonal events

Your Student Union should be thought of as a giant school disco and fittingly your Student Union will regularly host seasonal celebrations such as Christmas parties, Easter discos and summer balls. It is your duty to resemble an overexcited child at such events by dressing in appropriate fancy dress and eating and drinking until you are ill.

82. Wear fancy dress

As you reach the end of freshers' week, you will realise that students do not require a special occasion to wear fancy dress. As a result, most students wear fancy dress at least once a month. You should attempt to copy this trend. Popular costumes include:

✔ school uniforms

- ✔ nurses' uniforms
- ✔ bunny girl outfits
- ✔ togas
- ✔ FBI agents' gear

83. Watch stand-up comedy

The majority of Student Unions host regular comedy nights and you must endeavour to attend these events. The university comedy circuit offers students the opportunity to watch future comedy legends. It is also imperative that you take a seat near the front of the stage allowing yourself to be an easy target for the comedian who will no doubt mock your name, weight and home town.

84. Get banned from the Student Union

To maintain your student status, you should aim to be thrown out and barred from the Student Union at least once a year. One of the following is typically enough to secure at least a one week expulsion:

- ✗ urinate in a pint glass
- ✗ jump over the bar to pour your own pint
- ✗ vomit
- ✗ throw a pint over a band on stage
- ✗ fight with the bouncers
- ✗ steal a bar stool
- ✗ set off the fire alarm
- ✗ attempt to unscrew a plasma TV from the wall
- ✗ throw a pint on the DJ

85. Utilise the university fountain

Most universities have a fountain or a variety of water features and it is essential that you make full use of these following an evening at the Student Union. The most common activities involve:

- ✔ urinating
- ✔ skinny dipping
- ✔ washing clothes
- ✔ adding washing-up liquid
- ✔ adding pink food dye

86. Do a naked 400-metre run

The naked 400-metre sprint is a rite of passage for the majority of students. Whilst walking home from the Student Union it is essential that on at least three occasions you run around the athletic track naked. Boys must be fully naked whilst girls are allowed to wear either knickers or a bra. If both items are worn, you are automatically disqualified and you should attempt it again on a more drunken occasion.

87. Meet university security

The university security team is a strange collection of men who are usually in their late thirties or early forties and are suffering from premature greying. The majority of these men failed to join the police and could not survive as a door man. They believe that being a university security guard is the next best thing. It is a widely acknowledged fact that the university security team detests students and you should expect to clash over numerous road sign and trolley stealing episodes and an assortment of skinny dipping and initiation events.

88. Join a club or society

All universities have a freshers' fair in which you will have the opportunity to join any number of clubs and societies. It typically costs an annual fee of £40 to join a society and it is your duty to join at least three during your first year. As well as considering the more common clubs such as the rugby club, the drama society and the lesbian, gay and bisexual society, you should endeavour to join the more obscure clubs which are rapidly emerging such as the ultimate frisbee club, the hot air balloon society and the bobsleigh association. It is essential to note that few of these clubs will actually offer a chance to do their named activity but more positively they often offer free drinks.

89. Be initiated

To guarantee your position in a club or society you will need to be initiated. A student initiation is a rite of passage and it is likely that you will remember little about the experience. Nevertheless, it is a significant opportunity for you to prove your abilities and incapability. Most initiations involve:

✔ dirty pints
✔ naked 400-metre runs
✔ excessive vomiting

90. Wear university stash

University stash is clothing which associates you with a club or society. Your name or newly acquired nickname should be located on your back followed by an appropriate number. It is imperative that you wear this top with your flip flops and shorts on a daily basis and remember that it must only be washed on special occasions.

91. Go on a student demonstration

A demonstration provides the opportunity for you to make your views known and stand up for something you believe in. In contrast, a student demonstration is a fun free day out in which participants are commonly drunk, with the majority unsure about the reasons for the demonstration. However, throughout your time at university you should ensure that you participate in at least one demonstration each year so that you can one day tell your children about your fanatical demonstration days.

92. Take part in rag week

Rag week is a widely acknowledged student tradition. Surprisingly, rag week events commonly involve many of the popular student activities such as drinking, fancy dress and being pushed in a shopping trolley. However, in rag week you get the opportunity to do all of these things guilt free as you simultaneously raise money for charity.

93. Lose your student card

To gain access to your Student Union you must ensure that you carry your student card. Student cards typically feature an embarrassing photo of yourself with a ludicrous hair cut you tried out during your gap year. However, you will, on numerous occasions, lose this vital card. Your card may have been confiscated by your local post office because you repeatedly asked for a student discount, but most commonly you will have lost this card when skinny dipping in the fountain.

94. Visit the careers centre

Your Student Union careers centre should be your first port of call in the final year of your degree. This is not merely for career guidance but for the free tea and coffee, biscuits, pens and key rings which they offer.

Graduation

95. Cry on your last night

As you near the end of your university experience you should not be alarmed when you are overcome with emotion. Your final nights at university will be characterised by excessive drinking, excessive dancing and excessive emotion.

96. Reminisce

Your graduation celebrations will be accompanied by the increasing urge to reminisce and muse over your university experience. Looking back at your photographs and packing away your road signs and toga you will wonder where the last few years went with nostalgic amazement.

97. Add up your debt

As you stop reminiscing and begin looking to your future, you must be prepared that you will also be carrying a substantial amount of debt. You must try not to be depressed about this. Look at what you have to show for your debt: a degree, memories of the most amazing days of your life, and a giant indoor paddling pool.

98. Join the alumni

When you finally say goodbye to your university you must ensure that you join your university alumni. As well as informing you of important reunions, the alumni magazines give you the opportunity to see what your fellow graduates are doing. Be prepared to see students who were consistently drunk and dressed as FBI agents for three years now working for NASA and those who received first class degrees running charity shops in Slough.

99. Buy graduation photographs

Graduation is the ideal opportunity for your parents to confirm how proud they are that you actually managed to graduate. Most parents will insist on a graduation photograph and for this you must ensure that you look nothing like you have done for your entire degree. This photograph will then be given to all grandmothers and aunties who will display it proudly on their wall.

Please note: it is accepted that you will always hate this photograph.

100. Apply for a job

Applying for jobs is one of the negative aspects of graduation and whether you secure the ideal graduate job or end up working back in your local supermarket you should always be thinking about your next move. Graduate jobs are never for life but they do offer the ideal chance to meet a new bunch of friends and experience a toned-down version of university life.

Conclusion

101. Have the time of your life

Disregard what people say about school being the best years of your life: university wins this accolade. Where else are supposed adults allowed to drink excessive amounts whilst being dressed as golfers, vomiting over fruit machines, eating kebabs and getting pushed home in a shopping trolley on a nightly basis? University is truly character building. There are amazing times and low times and very rarely sober times, but if you survive it all you will join an elite club who has shared something special.

www.crombiejardine.com